Six-Word Lessons for
Transforming Conflict with Mindfulness

100 Lessons for More Presence and Skill in Resolving Conflicts

Judith Sugg, Ph.D.
Alisa Blum, MSW

Published by Pacelli Publishing
Bellevue, Washington

Six-Word Lessons for Transforming Conflict with Mindfulness
– Judith Sugg, Ph.D. and Alisa Blum, MSW

All rights reserved. No part of this book may be reproduced or transmitted in any form or by any means, electronic or mechanical including photocopying, recording or by any information storage or retrieval system, without the written permission of the publisher, except where permitted by law.

Limit of Liability: While the author and the publisher have used their best efforts in preparing this book, they make no representation or warranties with respect to accuracy or completeness of the content of this book. The advice and strategies contained herein may not be suitable for your situation. Consult with a professional when appropriate.

Copyright © 2016, 2017 by Judith Sugg, Ph.D. and Alisa Blum, MSW

Published by Pacelli Publishing
9905 Lake Washington Blvd. NE, #D-103
Bellevue, Washington 98004
PacelliPublishing.com

Cover and interior designed by Pacelli Publishing
Photo of Alisa Blum by Lester Tsai

ISBN-10: 1-933750-49-9
ISBN-13: 978-1-933750-49-1

What others say...

"Take a breath. Pause. Become a little more mindful. Learn to shift your style so that everybody wins. Nobody said it was easy. But it is definitely worth the work, for you, your friends, your associates, your boss and that special person in your life."

"This short read can change your life."
--Jerry Fletcher, Consultant to Consultants

"Mindfulness is powerful. With skilled leaders, I can learn steps fairly quickly and easily."

"Thank you...You found a way of pointing out simple but empowering tools to use on a day-to-day (maybe minute by minute) situation or problem."

"I enjoyed how you made the very intimidating concept of negotiating conflict accessible, doable, and not difficult to practice!"

"I thought of mindfulness as the opposite of conflict. Now I understand how I can be clearer and calmer even in tough situations."
--Workshop Participants

Six-Word Lessons for Transforming Conflict with Mindfulness

Table of Contents

When Our Goals and Emotions Clash 7

Developing Your Emotional Intelligence in Conflict........... 23

What is Your Go-To Style? 39

Practical Tools for Your Mindful Awareness 55

Practical Tools for Skillfully Negotiating Conflict 69

Practical Tools for Resolving Internal Conflict................... 85

Giving and Receiving Feedback with Grace........................ 95

Being Strategic: Taking Another Person's Perspective 103

Step into the Real Deal Now.. 109

Deep Breath! Putting it all Together 115

Six-Word Lessons for Transforming Conflict with Mindfulness

Six-Word Lessons for Transforming Conflict with Mindfulness

When Our Goals and Emotions Clash

Conflict is part of our lives.

Thank you for embarking on this important journey. Our intention with this book is simple:

- To help foster productive and creative interactions
- To lessen hurtful, disorienting conflict

We hope this book helps to hone your skills so you can engage creatively, respectfully, and gracefully in difficult situations.

We know conflict when it happens.

What is conflict? We know it when we see it! A useful definition is that conflict occurs when we aren't getting what we want--and we get emotional about it. By the time we get angry, fearful, irritated, or confused, our brain has triggered the body's alarm system: Danger!

And, we are now reacting out of old patterns.

And look at what it does.

This book focuses on work conflicts. How much wasted time is due to strained relationships and conflict at your work? A lot! It's been estimated that up to half of workplace problems stem from conflict and hostility--NOT deficits in skill or motivation.

When handled poorly, conflict costs time and energy. It results in costly turnover, and it ruins valued relationships.

Reactivity reduces our ability to choose.

How often have you said something (or done something) in the heat of the moment that you later regretted? This is reactivity. We react to a perceived threat with anger, hurt, fear, defensiveness, and hostility. Our heart races. Our jaw clenches. Our brain operates on emergency power, and our normal, thinking, resourceful self disappears.

Our power to reason and choose is greatly diminished.

What is in conflict? Our brains.

Our human, newer brain, developed over thousands of years to be smart, communicate, solve problems, plan, reflect, and manage. However, the older part of our brain is programmed to alert us to danger. Our bodies surge into high gear, and we spring into action. Our reasoning brain surrenders.

6

We lose our power to decide.

When we react, we lose our ability to think about priorities, values, and the long-term relationship. It's like we've boarded a train, and it's on one of these tracks: Fight, flight, or freeze. Like commuters, we usually ride the same route over and over. That's our pattern.

As you remember a conflict in your life, how did you react?

Why are we built this way?

Survival. In eras gone by, quick reactions meant we lived. We didn't have the luxury of figuring out if a rustle in the bushes meant a sparrow or a tiger. We had to act.

Our brains still operate in this ancient gear. Nowadays, we treat a confusing email like a death threat and hammer out an insulting answer.

We need alternatives.

Here's a simple definition of conflict

Conflict happens when we aren't getting what we need or want, and we have an emotional response. It only takes a moment for anger, disdain, irritation, or exasperation to skyrocket. The incident now takes on importance. Goals shift to defense, escape, or preparing for battle. The original issue may easily be forgotten.

How does conflict compare to negotiation?

All day long, people negotiate projects, hiring, salaries, chores, appointments, and purchases. When we negotiate, our goal stays central and emotions remain relatively neutral. Both parties have a stake in the outcome, and they are willing, up to a point, to work toward resolution. But if emotions start to flare, and the goal gets forgotten, we're back in conflict.

Where is that magic peace place?

There is no place on the planet without conflict. It happens on battlefields and in monasteries. It's part of being human.

But we need not be at the mercy of our reactions. As we try out new strategies, it is common to feel uncomfortable and even anxious. But discomfort simply means we are learning. These feelings won't kill us. War and stress can. If there is a magic sanctuary of peace, the seeds are inside us.

Is conflict valuable? Yes and no.

Does conflict have value?

Yes, when we need to react to danger.

Yes, when it's a signal (like anger) that something isn't right or we've been treated badly.

Yes, in productive conflict to find creative solutions.

And when is conflict not valuable?

When it devolves into continual fighting and an endless war.

When we freeze our positions and refuse to change.

When it escalates to something bigger and more painful.

When it ruins valued relationships.

When we are so fearful of conflict we hide who we are.

There is no "no conflict" zone.

Conflict conjures up the aggressive side of disagreements. But avoidance is an equally common behavior. While it seems like the easy way out at the time, it often just delays or compounds the problem. Chronic avoidance stems from fear. Chronic avoidance means we don't get what we need, and we don't respect our own values. The result is regret, resentment and discontent.

Being real: the value of speaking

When we articulate needs, wants, and desires, our interactions get clearer. Creative ideas surface. We build stronger teams. We accomplish more together as we meet challenges with openness and respect.

Will conflict still happen? Sure. But we do get better at managing ourselves. We listen for the signals, and we avoid knee-jerk reactions.

Our journey together in this book

This short book has the power to change behaviors and improve relationships--including your relationship with you.

Being *authentic* means finding a balance between self and the world. When we are fully present, open, and confident, we offer our unique self to the world. We are ready to receive what we need.

Developing Your Emotional Intelligence in Conflict

The emotional intelligence frame for conflict

Emotional intelligence is our skill-set for identifying our emotions, expressing ourselves, managing challenges, making tough decisions, and building relationships. In difficult situations, we need these skills to move past reactivity. By honing these skills, we build awareness. We manage ourselves and our stresses. We build strong relationships, make better decisions, and problem-solve creatively.

Conflicts are transformed with emotional intelligence.

Insight 1: When we pay attention to what's going on in our body (muscles, gut, heart racing, breathing), and our mind-chatter, then we learn our patterns. We are more present.

Insight 2: When we pay exquisite attention to the other person, we really hear them. We notice non-verbal cues. By suspending judgment, we start to understand their viewpoint. We are more flexible.

How do I develop self-awareness?

Are you living on autopilot? Then becoming more self-aware will feel like coming home.

When you regularly practice mindful pauses, you have more mental and physiological choice in what you do next. It's powerful.

Most of our clients can commit to a mindful pause because it is effective and possible in their busy day. The next lesson offers a simple body scan for awareness that you can do in one minute.

The one-minute scan for awareness

Let your shoulders drop.

Where do you feel the clothes touching skin?

Right now, where is the tension in your body. Scan through.

What is the taste in your mouth?

Where do you feel your breath?

If an emotion is present, where does it live in your body exactly? What are its qualities? On a scale of 1 to 10, how strong is it?

How do you decide your actions?

There are really just two ways to act.

- You react out of habit.
- You choose to act. You are self-aware, know what you want, and you stay alert to reactions of others. You develop the flexibility and grace to change when needed

Airplane pilots constantly correct course because they are aware and focused. We can be, too.

Six-Word Lessons for Transforming Conflict with Mindfulness

Why not go ahead and react?

Check out these common results:

I'm aggressive and people shy away from me.

I end up alone to avoid discomfort.

I give in but am resentful as heck about it.

I talk too much, nobody listens.

I fight, stalk off, blame, gossip, or backstab.

I give them the silent treatment. They give it back.

What are your wants and needs?

Understanding our goal makes for better decisions. Sharon's case is a good example:

George offers a great suggestion in a meeting. Sharon had the idea first and talked about earlier with George. She was waiting for the right time to bring it up, and George stole the moment.

Sharon is mad and not thinking clearly. She could just react. Or, better, she could step back and examine what she really wants.

So what does Sharon really want?

If Sharon takes a moment to slow things down and take a breath, she might find that what she really wants is credit for her idea. She also wants respect for her creativity. She wants to feel she is safe talking with a colleague and sharing ideas.

Sadly, Sharon didn't take that deep breath, and she reacted.

And how does reactivity show up?

If you were Sharon, how would you react?

__ Clam up and steam.

__ Give someone a piece of your mind.

__ Show your displeasure on your face.

__ Write a nasty email.

__ Plot revenge.

__ Take it to the boss.

__ Eat sugar or drink alcohol. Or both.

The familiar train to old places

What did Sharon do? She clammed up, got a headache, left work early, and started thinking about changing jobs.

To use a train metaphor, she boarded a train bound for escape and defeat. It felt familiar because patterns do feel familiar. But she didn't feel better.

Using your emotional intelligence for guidance

We asked Sharon a few questions to help her make a better choice.

What are you feeling? Stress, anger, hurt, or disappointment? Name it. What is going on in your body? Tension? Stomach knots? What is important, now and long-term? How does your (Sharon's) behavior contribute to the problem? (Unpleasant but true, our own behavior usually contributes.) What are two or three possible courses of action? What's the best action in this situation?

And isn't life just grand?

After Sharon clammed up, she had another opportunity to revisit her decision. This time, in a private meeting with her boss, he praised George's idea.

Sharon fumed inwardly, but her boss, a perceptive sort of guy, said, "What's up?" Sharon wanted to run from the room. Instead, she took a deep breath, decided to trust her boss, and said the following . . .

Being uncomfortable means change is possible.

"Listen, I should have spoken up in the meeting. It was my idea, and I shared it with George. I was shocked when he introduced it at the meeting as his own. I have been gritting my teeth about this for three wasted days. Usually I just clam up or leave. You know me pretty well, and I think you value me as a team-member. Can we talk about what I can do differently in the future?"

P.S. Sharon has already done something differently!

Practice becoming your own best coach.

Our emotional intelligence isn't fixed. It grows over a lifetime, especially when you commit to learning, reflecting, and using feedback. While a mentor can be a positive force for change, you can also be your own coach.

Think of a situation. Step back and gain perspective. Imagine you are a top coach, objective, neutral, and wise. Now write the answers to the questions in the next lesson as a coach.

Coaching questions to develop emotional intelligence

What am I feeling here?

What do I really want here?

What's important?

What would be my typical reaction?

What are some other creative possibilities?

What's the best choice or action?

Now, imagine that best choice happening.

Six-Word Lessons for Transforming Conflict with Mindfulness

What is Your Go-To Style?

A simple model for identifying style

Written assessments help identify conflict styles with precision. The following discussion is based on the Thomas-Kilmann conflict styles (see *Sources* at the end for information).

Most people can pick out their typical style just by reading these lessons. Are you a competitor and quick to act? Passive and avoiding? 50/50? Do you take time to hear everyone? Do you always say yes? You probably know!

Where does my style come from?

Before we start, you might be curious: where do we learn these patterns?

Parents and caregivers are our first models. If they were angry and aggressive, we may have adopted an aggressive style. Or we may do just the opposite--avoid and hide.

Little kids decide what is "normal" by what they see and hear. The old movie from childhood plays on until we update it.

Where else does it come from?

People often adopt the roles of their caretakers by gender. A girl might see her mother avoiding conflict or accommodating, for example, then model that as part of female behavior. What did your family model for you? Gender roles and stereotypes also live in books, movies, and media. When unchallenged, they guide our behavior unconsciously.

Groups have rules for handling conflicts.

Humans are constantly monitoring the norms of their group, whether the group is a family, school, sports team, work team or circle of friends. We assess our status, our safety and our role, and we pay attention to what is considered normal. We may pick up a group's style of conflict, at least short-term.

And how else did we learn?

Bullies learn that they feel good by having power over someone else. Shy people learn that hiding reduces their anxiety, at least short term. Confident people engage in collaborative discussions because the excitement and creativity of engagement feels invigorating.

When something works and feels good short-term, we tend to repeat it even if it is not an adequate solution all the time.

So isn't it all about winning?

Wanting to win is natural. But when a person constantly pushes their goal over other's needs and wants, they are aggressive. It's war, whether at home or in the office. "My way. I win. I have power over you."

In times of danger or crisis, aggressive command works. But the overuse of this strategy can also breed fear, intimidation, chronic stress, low productivity, poor relationships, lousy teams, and high turnover.

My natural inclination is toward avoidance.

Avoidance is a fear reaction. It works to reduce fear in the short-term, but over time it undercuts your power and will. As a style, a person appears passive or uninvolved, but they may feel scared and hesitant.

Avoid a conflict when it doesn't really matter. Your spouse is wearing that weird shirt--is the battle worth it? Your team wants Chinese food--maybe just say yes? But engage when it is important. Your creativity and input is needed.

Big fear: they won't like me.

Chronic avoidance is bowing to fear.

We've found that the fear of "they won't like me any more if …" drives a lot of avoidance. In the extreme, it eats away at self-esteem. It inhibits performance at work. It may manifest as addiction, underhanded manipulation, or physical stress and illness.

Not a good strategy over time.

To change or not to change?

Are you a chronic avoider? Good news: You can change and it's worth it.

Bad news? You'll be uncomfortable in the beginning as you stretch past your comfort zone. You may say too much, or say it awkwardly, or blurt it out. People may not like it. They may judge. But you'll start to get yourself back. You'll improve.

The world needs your voice, too.

I like to split the difference.

Compromise is a good decision at times-- especially when the important issues are decided and you're finishing the details.

Why do we compromise? It feels fair. It takes so little work or reflection.

When is it a poor strategy? When the decision is important, or when it is our only strategy. Most important negotiations need more thought. Don't be lazy; not everything is 50/50.

Here, I'll do it for you!

Accommodating also has its place. If you work for a busy person and they ask you to do something, accommodating them is part of your job. If your friend asks you to help him hold up a bank, and you do it—well ...

Accommodating, like avoidance, can lead to passivity and a loss of self. And, it can lead to revenge and nastiness when you've had enough. This style has to do with expected roles and norms. Make sure the norms make sense for the situation.

I win, you win, we win.

It's easy to see the joy and beauty in this style and the win/win approach. It is a thing of beauty when the stakes are important, the stakeholders have different needs, and when the results will last a long time.

A true win/win situation addresses values and needs at a deeper level. The process can take time, but people leave feeling they have been heard and their message honored. They value the conclusion and relationships.

Is win/win the real answer?

Collaboration takes people skills, practice, patience, and inherent respect for participants. It requires willingness and intention. Use it when stakes are high and relationships are valued. Good teams, good marriages, and good companies value win/win for the results and the buy-in.

However, collaborating for 30 minutes about lunch? Or with your six-year-old on bedtime? Not so much. Use collaboration when it matters.

Here's your quick and dirty assessment.

Be your own consultant. Think of recent conflicts and for each one, ask:

Did you go for the win? Run away? Say yes without thinking? Did you split the difference? Did you take time to consider all sides? What was your goal/need in the situation? Did your strategy work in working toward your goal? Is your relationship better? Worse? The same?

What might have worked even better?

Six-Word Lessons for Transforming Conflict with Mindfulness

Practical Tools for Your Mindful Awareness

The pause that makes a difference

When we react emotionally in a conflict, we abandon our choices. We feel like a victim. We may react with blame, criticism, and labeling.

Mindfulness tools are simply pauses. They act on that space between our brain going "HIGH ALERT!" and our next move. They make a difference because they provide the moment to choose.

The best basic tool: your breath

We're not telling you to sit in full lotus position and meditate for an hour. But breath does have immense power to help us shift states, redirect thoughts, and decide what we really want.

Using breath as a pause helps us switch from a primitive, reactive brain to a thinking, adult brain.

A breath tool: try it now.

Take a breath, exhale completely.

Exhale a second time and empty the lungs entirely.

Breathe in fully and hold briefly .

When you exhale, just let it go.

Check the difference.

Another breath tool to practice now

Need some courage or strength?

Pull your belly in slightly.

Breathe sideways into your ribcage.

Exhale slowly, with control.

Try five to seven breaths, then check your state and emotions.

This breath is called Warrior Breath for a reason!

Is your body enemy or friend?

When we react, we are on automatic pilot. We think we need to react immediately. Not true! Unless safety is a factor, take a moment to move--literally. Lift your shoulders, drop them, and breathe. Stand up and walk. Stretch. These few moments are gold.

50

Shoulders are where we hold tension.

This is true for everyone in stress: We tense our shoulders. This affects our jaw, neck, and back, too. Simply relaxing our shoulders may not solve all problems but it does help.

How do you relax your shoulders easily? You might be able to just notice and relax. The next lesson has more suggestions.

51

So relax those poor tense shoulders.

Lift your shoulders up toward your ears on an inhale.

Slowly let them roll back and down on exhale. Remember to time it with your breath.

Repeat a few times.

Then do some shoulder rolls from front to back.

Check your state--amazing, isn't it?

To be kind, help your neck.

Drop your chin to your chest.

Roll to the right on an inhale, hold a breath.

Drop down on exhale, roll to left on inhale, and hold.

Avoid rolling back—it is hard on the neck.

An easy body scan for awareness

Shift into what is happening now with these simple steps:

Where do you feel your breath--right now?

What is the taste in your mouth? Where in your mouth?

What sounds do you hear in the room?

Can you feel your heart or hear your heart?

How to get yourself to practice

If you practice simple mindful techniques even for brief periods, over time, you will gain more control over your state and reactions. Judy started practicing these techniques every time she rode an elevator at work, which was six to seven times a day. By associating a regular activity with the mindful technique, it was easy for her to remember to drop her shoulders and take a slow breath. It helped her meetings, too!

Make mindful breaks part of life.

The trick is to time your mindful pause to something you already do anyway. Do you talk on the phone often? Then every time you hang up, give a little body shake, take a deep breath, and taste the taste in your mouth.

Ground yourself from the feet up.

Be more centered in just 30 seconds by following these steps:

Feel your feet as they touch the floor.

Open your ears, letting sounds flow through without comment.

See something close to you. Now look at something far away.

Note the taste in your mouth.

Feel your breath move through your body.

Practical Tools for Skillfully Negotiating Conflict

You can influence yourself and others.

Do you believe you can change? Shift from reaction to purpose? Do you have the skill to really gauge what is happening with others? Can you learn to read beneath the surface?

The first step is trusting that you can get better; we all can. This attitude or mindset drives success--if we think we can, we usually can.

Just give me the data, please.

Try playing consultant to yourself, and being curious. Remember a recent conflict. What happened inside? Thoughts, sensations, heat, racing mind, tension, holding your breath? Did your heart rate rise? Did you talk too much or clam up? Did you say yes when wanted to say no?

We encourage you to be curious! Be a neutral observer. Take a baseline of your own reactions.

I start to see red and...

Getting mad? Here are some helpful tips:

Move or shift to release tension.

Count to ten. Better yet, count backwards from 75 by twos. Why? Different part of your brain. Engaging the logical part of your brain helps emotions recede.

Take some slow breaths with slower exhales.

Walk, move, or leave saying, "I need ten minutes."

If the other person is angry, suggest a break. Safety is a priority.

Pay attention to words you choose.

The words you choose when you communicate with others can make or break a conversation. Consider the impact, for example, of changing, "You're wrong" to, "Can I share my perspective?"

The next time you are in conflict with someone, take a timeout and plan how to express yourself in the most effective manner possible.

Please pay attention to your safety.

If you need to confront someone who may be volatile, put a plan in place to keep yourself safe. For example, if you are at work, make sure someone with authority is aware of the situation.

Consider whether you should be alone with this person. Make sure someone is nearby in case an intervention is needed.

Take a break when feeling stuck.

You may find yourself at an impasse when trying to resolve a conflict. Give yourself and the other person permission to take a break. Don't put off resuming your negotiation for too long. Decide whether you need a few hours or maybe a day.

Sometimes all you need is a little more time.

Increase your confidence with self-talk.

You will more effectively handle difficult situations by giving yourself messages like, "I've effectively handled situations like this before" or "I now have the skills to communicate my needs."

Write a list of messages that will help you have the confidence to successfully resolve a conflict.

Have positive thoughts about the outcome.

We often anticipate the worst when we have to deal with a conflict.

Instead, imagine in detail how well your interaction with this person could go. Write it down. You will find that having positive thoughts will keep you calm and more confident. And you will be more likely to have a positive outcome.

Are your expectations of others realistic?

Sometimes it is difficult to resolve conflicts if you expect others to give in to all of your requests or if you have excessively high expectations of their behavior. Take some time to consider what you can realistically expect from others. Think about your priorities and consider what expectations you can release and what expectations are critical for you.

Do you give in too much?

Whether or not you identified "accommodating" as part of your style, you may find that you do give in a lot. Why? Are you afraid to disappoint people? Are you fearful of others reactions?

Alternatively, share what's important to you. "I know you want me to finish this project. It's important that I also honor my commitments to Trish." Allow others to understand your needs.

Do not try resolving conflicts online.

It's tempting to try to resolve conflicts online. While it can feel safer not to face the other person directly, resolving conflicts online may create more problems.

When you can't hear the other person's tone of voice or see facial expressions, it's hard to develop rapport. Research tells us that we think we are interpreting their tone correctly, but we are often wrong. Don't act on wrong information.

Do you often dominate the conversation?

Do you tend to talk more than you listen?

If you do, try doing the opposite. This may go against your natural tendencies but try to listen more than you talk. You may be surprised at what you learn and the rapport you gain.

Having relationships: the value of listening

The NUMBER ONE skill in conflict resolution, and maybe in relationships as whole, is listening. Listening to understand means we clear our own head of assumptions and conversation (as much as possible) and try to really hear what is going on with the other person--in words, tone, body language, and emotions.

The conversation in our head changes.

When we listen with the qualities of emotional intelligence, we observe our own emotional state with curiosity. By keeping self-talk and judgment at bay, we more clearly sense what is happening with others. We sort out what the real issue is and stay focused and centered. We influence events in alignment with our goals and values.

A guide for listening to understand

Start by practicing good listening skills with someone you like.

In a conversation, listen so intently that you could repeat back exactly what they said if needed. What are their key words? What tone of voice and gestures do they use?

Talk ten percent of the time. Pause. Breathe. Do NOT give advice, or tell a similar story, or do "one better". Listen.

Practical Tools for Resolving Internal Conflict

Yes, conflict starts inside of us.

Internal conflict is the pull we feel when we have two different needs.

We want to act, but we don't. We want to be confident, but our knees shake. We want to move, but we stay in the same place. We want to eat better, but we snack on cake.

Here are some strategies to explore to make peace with yourself.

Are you your own worst enemy?

Do you find that you are more critical of yourself than others are of you? This may be a result of internalizing negative messages you received as a child. You can turn this around by becoming aware of these messages. Consciously substitute negative messages about yourself with positive self-messages.

You can! It is your mind.

Can you forgive the other person?

It's easy to hold a grudge against someone with whom you have had conflict. Unfortunately, grudges can be quite destructive--destroying families, friendships, and workplaces. Forgive the other person when you can.

If you can't resolve a conflict with someone, change the context of the relationship by creating some emotional distance. And move on.

Are you worrying yourself too much?

You may find that fretting about what could go wrong keeps you from directly dealing with a conflict. Often, worries about what could go wrong are exaggerated.

Talk with someone you trust and who is familiar with the situation. You may find that the reality of the situation is less toxic than your fears.

# What are your early warning signals?

How does your body react when you are in internal conflict? Does your heart beat fast, do your hands get sweaty, do you clench your jaw, does your stomach tighten? Do you talk to yourself--in a nasty tone?

By paying attention to your early warning signals, you can start to redirect and calm yourself.

Increase your confidence with self-talk.

You will handle difficult situations more effectively if you shift your self-talk to messages like, "I've effectively handled situations like this before" or, "I now have the skills to communicate my needs." Write a list of messages that will help you have the confidence to successfully resolve this conflict. Move from inner conflict to being more congruent.

What causes fighting and bickering inside?

Most of us are chock full of conflicting desires. We want to lose five pounds, but that pizza sounds good. We want to get up early, but we stay up watching a movie. We want to stand up for ourselves, but we give in when there is resistance.

We rarely take the time to unscramble this stuff non-judgmentally.

Take out a sheet of paper.

For an internal conflict or decision, write:

On one hand, I want _____. What this choice does for me is _____. This is important because _____.

On the other hand, I also want _____. What this choice does for me is _____. This is important because _____.

Collaborate with yourself. What creative solution honors the different needs best?

Our outside actions mirror our insides.

It's a frightening thought, isn't it? We thought those internal conflicts were, well, hidden from everyone.

Not true. Others see internal conflict in our expressions and behavior. The good news is that as we reflect, decide, and put an action plan into place, our congruence and clarity start to show up on the outside.

Six-Word Lessons for Transforming Conflict with Mindfulness

Giving and Receiving Feedback with Grace

81

Listen to understand all the layers.

Feedback can be the source of fear and conflict. We offer what we think is feedback, and we get anger back in return. Or someone gives us feedback, and we feel hurt or insulted. Yet, feedback is how we get better. It is a step in clearing the air, and it is part of all work environments.

Feedback is not created equally. Learning to listen, take the gems and leave the dregs, and learning to offer feedback artfully can further your career.

Appreciation is your best next step.

Never underestimate the power of appreciation! It sets the tone for a productive conversation. The next time you need to work out a conflict with someone, start by letting him or her know how much you appreciate their willingness to work things out with you.

The best outcome: continue the conversation.

It is often difficult to resolve a conflict in one sitting, particularly in complex situations. Be realistic about what you can expect.

Consider it a success when both parties agree to continue the conversation. A short space of time between discussions can help open up perspectives. At the very least, emotional charge decreases.

Accept negative feedback without becoming defensive.

It's natural to want to defend yourself when hearing negative feedback. The next time you get feedback that is difficult to hear, think about whether there is some validity to this feedback. Think about how you can use this feedback as an opportunity to grow.

Use empathy when giving constructive feedback.

Put yourself in the other person's shoes. Imagine what it would feel like to be in their situation. Reflect this sense of understanding when you give your feedback. Giving constructive feedback with empathy shows that you care.

When people feel cared about they are much more likely to pay attention to your feedback.

Remember the importance of positive feedback.

Your discussions will be more productive if you infuse the conversations with positive feedback. This is particularly helpful when starting and ending a conversation about a conflict you are trying to resolve.

Statements such as, "I value our relationship" or "Thank you for hearing me out" will make the other person much more receptive to your communication.

Being Strategic: Taking Another Person's Perspective

How do you see the situation?

In conflict, your perspective is, by definition, different from the other person's.

Both of you have feelings, desires, and maybe your self-esteem at stake. Being strategic in resolving conflict means being self-aware, but also "other aware", too. It doesn't mean you have to agree, but knowing where the other person is coming from is valuable and humanizing.

Be strategic: step in their shoes.

Start with yourself: What causes you to view the situation this way? How does your culture, personality, or circumstance show up?

Now imagine the other person: What do you know about them? Their values? Position? What is important to them?

What shows up about their culture, personality, or circumstances?

Communicate your understanding of their perspective.

To understand another's perspective we must be willing to suspend our own opinions and then look at the world through their eyes. What are the pressures in their life? What is driving their behavior and attitude?

When we gain this type of insight, we more easily diffuse the tension. By small indications of understanding like, "I'm guessing you are under pressure because of the deadline," we create space to maneuver.

Judgments halt discussion and inflame conflict.

Taking the other's perspective is a powerful strategy for sidestepping the judgments that block effective communication. Carrie and Maria are on a team. Carrie is frustrated. She thinks (judges) that Maria is a pushover and scared to speak up. As Carrie reflects, she realizes that Maria is reserved by nature, conscious of status, and may feel it's inappropriate to assert herself. With that understanding, Carrie can communicate her needs in a more positive way.

The hardest part is our willingness.

Sometimes it is hard to admit that the other person is just as committed to their position as you are to yours. They are not misguided or bad or silly, they just are different. They have different needs.

It takes maturity and emotional intelligence to stick with the issues and not go personal. Glimpsing the other person's perspective, if only for a moment, humanizes all of us.

Step into the Real Deal Now

Practice with memories of old conflicts.

Whether at home or at work, opportunities for practice are not hard to find. Start by analyzing past conflicts:

What happened? What was the issue or content?

Did I feel judged? Did I judge the other?

Did I react out of old habits?

What worked? What did I do well?

What could I do differently?

Practice your skills in the moment.

The next time you witness any conflict, PAUSE!

What is happening in your body?

Where are your shoulders?

How is your breath?

Now, what is working here?

What could you do better?

94

Practice with on-going difficult situations.

Think about an on-going difficult situation. An aggressive team member? A bulldozer? A teenager giving you the silent treatment?

What is happening in your body, shoulders, and breath? What's your self-talk? What do you want for yourself in this situation? What's driving the other person's behavior?

Realistically, what strategies can you employ here? You do have choices. What are they?

95

Practice skills by imagining future situations.

Play it out in your mind. Imagine what to do the next time. Now, take a deep breath, count to five, let the air out slowly.

Where is the other person coming from? What is the issue here? Do you have any mind chatter or judgments that get in your way? What is your best action here? Your best words?

Try it out, revise. After all, this is in the privacy of your own mind.

Six-Word Lessons for Transforming Conflict with Mindfulness

Deep Breath! Putting it all Together

96

The incalculable importance of transforming conflict

It is our firm belief that the world needs more people, like you, willing to move from old-style reaction into discussion, resolution, graceful acceptance, gratitude, awareness, and understanding.

You are a part of this. Your willingness to change and grow is an example to those at work, in your home, and in your community.

Many opportunities to hone our skills

Conflict is. It won't go away as long as we are different from each other. Would we want it any other way? Our skill in conflict, however, can improve. Our next hint involves how to utilize feedback and handle self-critiques.

Reflecting on difficult situations helps learning

After a conflict or episode:

Stand in a quiet place.

Start the "movie" where the conflict started.

Note your own movements, words, and reactions.

What is your part of the dance? What is their part?

What goes well?

# 99

The important question to ask yourself

And now….

What is one thing you could do differently to improve? (Even just breathing more!)

Take this idea and run it through your mind. What you practice is what you'll get in the future. Make it something better.

100

Growing in confidence, appreciation, and wisdom

What do you appreciate about what you bring to your team? To your work? To your family? Your friends?

Knowing your strengths and gifts is a part of real confidence. Confidence, and adjusting your behavior based on your own and others' feedback, will give you wisdom for your next difficult discussion.

Sources

Crum, T. (1987). *The Magic of Conflict.* New York: Touchstone.

Eunson, B. (2012). *Conflict Management.* Milton, Australia: Wiley.

Goleman, D. (2000). *Working with Emotional Intelligence.* New York: Bantam.

Marturano, J. (2014). *Finding the Space to Lead.* New York: Bloomsbury Press.

Patterson, K., Grenny, J., McMillan, R, Switzler, A. (2005). *Crucial Confrontations.* New York: McGraw-Hill.

Rock, D. (2009). *Your Brain at Work.* New York: HarperCollins.

Tan, C. (2012). *Search Inside Yourself.* New York: HarperCollins.

Thomas-Kilmann *Conflict Mode Instrument* at KilmannDiagnostics.com.

Online (and free) conflict styles assessment at BuildingPeace.org/conflict-styles

Judith Sugg, Ph.D., is co-director at AIM for Organizational Health. AIM supports organizations with mindfulness, communication, and conflict resolution tools to increase individual and organizational success. Her background in business management and psychology is supplemented by 20-plus years of teaching mindfulness practices.

Alisa Blum, MSW, is principal consultant at Alisa Blum & Associates, a training consulting and coaching company specializing in improving individual and organizational performance. She co-directs AIM for Organizational Health, providing mindfulness programs to decrease stress and enhance conflict resolution. Alisa's background includes positions as a psychotherapist and as a training director.

AIM for Organizational Health

aimportland@gmail.com

AIMPortland.com

About the *Six-Word Lessons* Series

Legend has it that Ernest Hemingway was challenged to write a story using only six words. He responded with the story, "For sale: baby shoes, never worn." The story tickles the imagination. Why were the shoes never worn? The answers are left up to the reader's imagination.

This style of writing has a number of aliases: postcard fiction, flash fiction, and micro fiction. Lonnie Pacelli was introduced to this concept in 2009 by a friend, and started thinking about how this extreme brevity could apply to today's communication culture of text messages, tweets and Facebook posts. He wrote the first book, *Six-Word Lessons for Project Managers*, then started helping other authors write and publish their own books in the series.

The books all have six-word chapters with six-word lesson titles, each followed by a one-page description. They can be written by entrepreneurs who want to promote their businesses, or anyone with a message to share.

See the entire *Six-Word Lessons* Series at **6wordlessons.com**

www.ingramcontent.com/pod-product-compliance
Lightning Source LLC
Chambersburg PA
CBHW062009070426
42451CB00008BA/294